I0815584

The Incredible Inclined Plane

Julie Murray

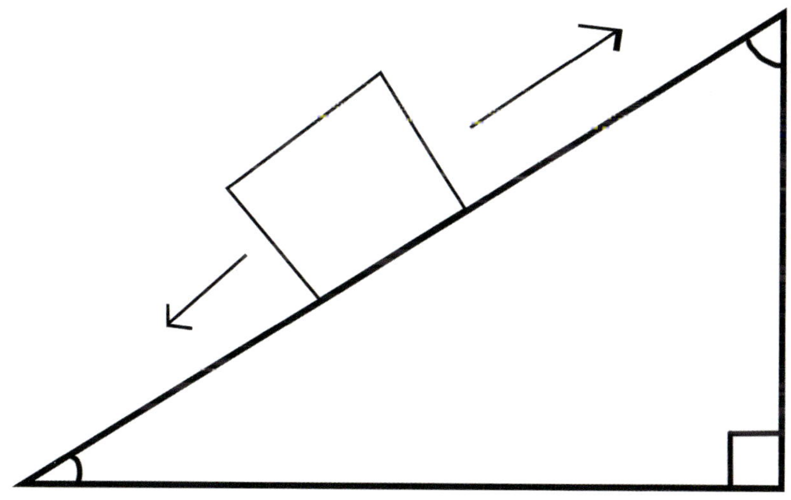

Abdo Kids Junior
is an Imprint of Abdo Kids
abdobooks.com

abdobooks.com

Published by Abdo Kids, a division of ABDO, P.O. Box 398166, Minneapolis, Minnesota 55439.

Abdo Kids Junior™ is a trademark and logo of Abdo Kids.

Printed in the United States of America, North Mankato, Minnesota.

052024

092024

Photo Credits: Getty Images, Shutterstock

Production Contributors: Teddy Borth, Jennie Forsberg, Grace Hansen

Design Contributors: Candice Keimig, Pakou Moua

Library of Congress Control Number: 2023948558

Publisher's Cataloging-in-Publication Data

Names: Murray, Julie, author.

Title: The incredible inclined plane / by Julie Murray

Description: Minneapolis, Minnesota : Abdo Kids, 2025 | Series: Simple machines | Includes online resources and index.

Identifiers: ISBN 9798384900597 (lib. bdg.) | ISBN 9798384901297 (ebook) | ISBN 9798384901648 (Read-to-me eBook)

Subjects: LCSH: Simple machines--Juvenile literature. | Inclined planes--Juvenile literature. | Ramps--Juvenile literature. | Slides--Juvenile literature. | Machinery--Juvenile literature. | Hand tools--Juvenile literature.

Classification: DDC 621.8--dc23

Table of Contents

The Incredible Inclined Plane

An inclined plane is also called a ramp. It is a simple machine.

It is used to move objects to higher or lower places.

7

A ramp is a flat surface.

It has no moving parts.

A ramp has three sides.

The sides form a triangle.

slant length
rise
run

One side is the longest.

It is also sloped.

Force is needed to move a **load**.

load
force
gravity

A ramp helps spread the **force** out.

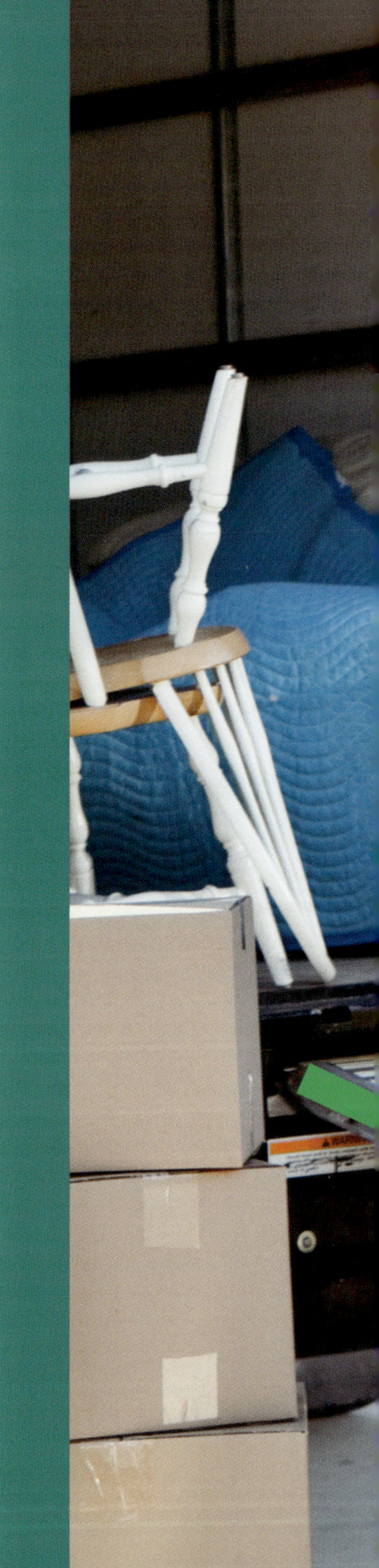

load
force
gravity

Less **force** is needed to move the **load**.

A ramp makes moving
a **load** easier!

Inclined Planes Around You

wheelchair ramp

slanted roof

slide

stairs

Glossary

force
power, energy, or physical strength.

load
an amount of something carried.

Index

Visit **abdokids.com** to access crafts, games, videos, and more!

Use Abdo Kids code

STK0597

or scan this QR code!